PUERTO RICO

ALASKA

CANADA

PACIFIC
OCEAN

UNITED
STATES

HAWAII

PUERTO
RICO

MEXICO

PUERTO RICO

HELLO
U.S.A.

by Joyce Johnston

Lerner Publications Company

You'll find this picture of a coral reef at the beginning of every chapter. The coral and sponges are found near Desecheo, a small island about 14 miles from the island of Puerto Rico. Desecheo, like the rest of Puerto Rico, is surrounded by colorful coral reefs, making it an exciting destination for divers.

Cover (left): Waterfall in El Yunque rain forest. Cover (right): Calle Cristo in Old San Juan. Pages 2–3: Puerto Ricans relax at Sun Bay Beach on Vieques Island. Page 3: Neighborhood near Old San Juan.

This book is available in two editions:
Library binding by Lerner Publications Company, a division of Lerner Publishing Group
Soft cover by First Avenue Editions, an imprint of Lerner Publishing Group
241 First Avenue North
Minneapolis, MN 55401 U.S.A.

Website address: www.lernerbooks.com

Library of Congress Cataloging-in-Publication Data

Johnston, Joyce, 1958–
    Puerto Rico / by Joyce Johnston. (Revised and expanded 2nd edition)
        p.   cm. — (Hello U.S.A.)
    Includes index.
    ISBN: 0–8225–4058–4 (lib. bdg. : alk. paper)
    ISBN: 0–8225–4150–5 (pbk. : alk. paper)
        1. Puerto Rico—Juvenile literature. [1. Puerto Rico.] I. Title. II. Series.
    F1958.3 .J65 2002
    972.95—dc21   2001000329

Manufactured in the United States of America
1 2 3 4 5 6 – JR – 07 06 05 04 03 02

CONTENTS

Puerto Rico is Spanish for "rich port." The island's white-sand beaches and warm weather have appealed to visitors for centuries.

THE LAND

Island of Enchantment

illions of years ago, a chain of mountains southeast of Florida connected the eastern coast of North America with the northern coast of South America. Over time, the oceans rose and covered much of the land. Just the tops of these mountains still poke above the water, forming a string of islands about 2,000 miles long. The island chain, called the West Indies, stretches from Florida to Venezuela, in northern South America. Because they separate the Atlantic Ocean from the Caribbean Sea, the West Indies are sometimes called the Caribbean islands.

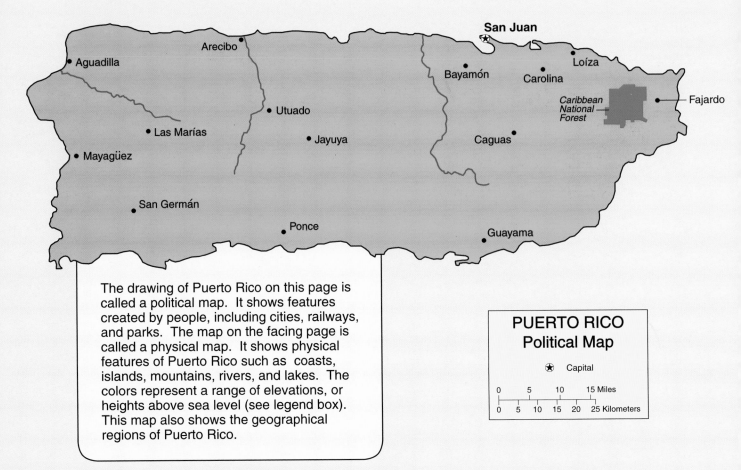

Aguadilla

Arecibo

San Juan

Bayamón

Loíza

Carolina

Caribbean National Forest

Fajardo

Utuado

Las Marías

Jayuya

Caguas

Mayagüez

San Germán

Ponce

Guayama

The drawing of Puerto Rico on this page is called a political map. It shows features created by people, including cities, railways, and parks. The map on the facing page is called a physical map. It shows physical features of Puerto Rico such as coasts, islands, mountains, rivers, and lakes. The colors represent a range of elevations, or heights above sea level (see legend box). This map also shows the geographical regions of Puerto Rico.

PUERTO RICO
Political Map

⭐ Capital

0	5	10	15 Miles

0	5	10	15	20	25 Kilometers

ATLANTIC OCEAN

DOMINICAN
REPUBLIC

Desecheo
Island

Culebrinas River

Arecibo River

COASTAL LOWLANDS

La Plata River

FOOTHILLS

CENTRAL

MOUNTAINS

El Yunque

SIERRA DE
LUQUILLO

Cerro de Punta

COASTAL VALLEYS

FOOTHILLS

CORDILLERA CENTRAL

COASTAL VALLEYS

Mona Passage

COASTAL LOWLANDS

Mona
Island

Culebra
Island

Vieques
Island

Mosquito Bay

Caribbean Sea

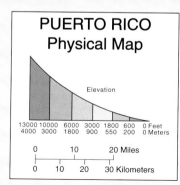

PUERTO RICO
Physical Map

Elevation

| 13000 | 10000 | 6000 | 3000 | 1800 | 600 | 0 Feet |
| 4000 | 3000 | 1800 | 900 | 550 | 200 | 0 Meters |

0   10   20 Miles

0   10   20   30 Kilometers

Among these islands lies the **Commonwealth** of Puerto Rico. As a commonwealth, Puerto Rico governs itself but also belongs to the United States. The Puerto Ricans living on the island are U.S. citizens. They enjoy certain privileges, such as military protection, and economic assistance from the United States.

Puerto Rico is made up of one large island and a number of smaller islands nearby. The large island is called Puerto Rico. Mona, Vieques, and Culebra are the largest of the other islands.

Puerto Rico's nearest neighbors are the Virgin Islands and the island of Hispaniola, which is shared by two countries—Haiti and the Dominican Republic. The Virgin Islands lie east of Puerto Rico across a strip of water called the Virgin Passage. Hispaniola is west of Puerto Rico across the Mona Passage.

The island of Vieques is home to this quiet country inn.

The island of Puerto Rico has four land regions. They are the Coastal Lowlands, the Foothills, the Central Mountains, and the Coastal Valleys. The Coastal Lowlands—two long, flat belts of land about 10 miles wide—run along Puerto Rico's northern and southern coasts. Puerto Rico's largest cities are built on the Coastal Lowlands. Farms and sandy beaches are found on this part of the island, too.

The Foothills rise from the Coastal Lowlands toward the center of the island. At their lowest point, these hills rise only about 100 feet. Farther inland they reach 700 feet in height.

Palm trees and many other plants thrive along the Coastal Lowlands.

The peaks of the Cordillera Central rise along Puerto Rico's center like a backbone.

The rugged peaks of the Central Mountains tower over the other land regions of Puerto Rico. A long, narrow mountain range—called the Cordillera Central—runs nearly the entire length of the island from west to east. Farmers grow coffee and fruit in the valleys between the steep mountain slopes. Cerro de Punta, the highest point on Puerto Rico, reaches 4,389 feet in the Central Mountains. A small mountain range called Sierra de Luquillo rises in the eastern part of the region.

On the eastern and western coasts of Puerto Rico lie the Coastal Valleys. On a map, the valleys seem to poke into the mountains like fingers. Farmers grow coconuts and other fruits as well as sugarcane in these low, fertile areas.

A stream rolls through the Foothills at the base of the Sierra de Luquillo.

Thousands of rivers and streams spill down Puerto Rico's mountainsides. The island's waterways are short and shallow, so large boats cannot travel up or down them. Puerto Rico's major rivers include the Arecibo, La Plata, and Culebrinas Rivers.

Most of the time, Puerto Rico's tropical weather is warm and calm. The average temperature in January is 73° F. In July it's a comfortable 80° F. Because the temperature almost never drops below 60° F, no snow falls on Puerto Rico—not even in the mountains.

Rainfall is plentiful on the northern half of Puerto Rico, which receives about 70 inches of rain each year. As much as 200 inches drench the **tropical rain forest** of El Yunque each year. The southern part of the island is drier, receiving only about 37 inches of rain yearly.

June through November is hurricane season in the West Indies. A hurricane, or severe tropical storm with strong winds and driving rains, lashes Puerto Rico about once every 10 years. In September 1989, Hurricane Hugo killed 12 Puerto Ricans and destroyed $1 billion worth of property on the island. Another storm, Hurricane Georges, struck the islands in 1998. Fortunately, Georges wasn't as severe as Hugo.

The high winds and heavy rains of Hurricane Hugo flattened thousands of trees and destroyed many homes on Puerto Rico.

Wildflowers, such as these golden trumpets, dot the Puerto Rican countryside.

Lush forests and wild plants once covered Puerto Rico. But by the mid-1900s, settlers had cut down most of the plants and trees to make room for farms. Only a few of the original forests remain. El Yunque rain forest is home to trees such as the *palo colorado*, the *tabanuco*, and the sierra palm.

Although the island has fewer forests than it once had, many types of trees and plants grow there. The dry climate of southern Puerto Rico makes the area well suited for cactuses and bunchgrass. Palm trees, mangroves, and huge ceiba (silk-cotton or kapok) trees are just a few of the hundreds of kinds of trees that grow on the island. Hibiscus, poinsettias, and other colorful flowers also brighten the landscape.

One of Puerto Rico's smallest animals is the *coquí*. This tan-colored frog grows to only 1 inch in length and clings to damp leaves throughout the island. The coquí's two-note croak sounds like a bird's song. Other animals that live on Puerto Rico include snakes, iguanas, Puerto Rican parrots, and many other colorful birds that are found nowhere else in the United States.

The tiny coquí *(right)* hops among the leaves. Coral reefs *(above),* home to many colorful fish and plants, ring Puerto Rico.

THE HISTORY

Caribbean Commonwealth

hrieking parrots, thundering waves, and other wild noises of the forest and ocean were probably the only sounds on Puerto Rico 3,000 years ago. No human voices echoed through the island's valleys or drifted across its beaches.

No one is really sure when the first people landed on Puerto Rico. But at least 1,000 years ago, American Indians canoed north from what later became Venezuela. Island by island, the Indians traveled farther until they had explored and settled many Caribbean islands of the West Indies.

The Arawak, who probably disappeared around A.D. 600, left little behind. Some of their work, such as these rock carvings, remains on islands throughout the West Indies.

In Taino villages, houses made from palm tree trunks surrounded central squares.

The first Indians to live on Puerto Rico were part of a group known as the Arawak. They formed beautiful pots from clay and painted them red and white. The Arawak made their homes on the island until around A.D. 600. Then they disappeared, although no one is sure why. Some experts believe that they died or fled war or disease.

By A.D. 1000, another group of people called the Taino were living on Puerto Rico and other islands of the West Indies. The Taino set up villages ruled by a *cacique*, or chief. The Indians built round houses by lining up the trunks of palm trees in a circle, then topping them with cone-shaped roofs. At night the Taino slept in hammocks. During the day, they hunted, fished, and farmed.

Researchers discovered this Taino ballpark *(below)* at the town of Utuado. In the game played here, players used any part of their bodies, except their hands, to keep the ball in the air.

The Taino made drawings on rocks uncovered near the ballpark *(above).*

The Taino delivered their crops to a village storage center after each harvest.

One of the Taino's most important crops was the yucca plant. The Indians ground the roots of this plant into flour for making bread called *cassava*. Taino farmers also grew corn, potatoes, beans, peanuts, peppers, cotton, and tobacco. For meat the Taino hunted iguanas and small, furry animals called *hutias*. Along the coasts, fishers gathered sea turtles, clams, snails, and a variety of fish to eat.

The Taino called Puerto Rico Borinquén, which means "land of the brave lord" in their language. And Taino, their name for themselves, means "gentle." As the name suggests, the Taino were peaceful people.

But in the 1400s, their peace came to an end. The Taino's way of life was destroyed with the arrival of two new groups— the Carib Indians and the Spaniards. Like the Taino, the Caribs came to the West Indies from South America. They settled on nearby islands and frequently attacked the Taino— sometimes capturing Taino women and destroying villages.

Skillful warriors, the Carib Indians fought many wars against the Taino.

Spain laid claim to Puerto Rico in 1493, when explorer Christopher Columbus landed on the island. Fifteen years later, Juan Ponce de León established a Spanish **colony,** or settlement, on Puerto Rico.

A year after Christopher Columbus *(holding flag)* first arrived in America, he landed on the island of Puerto Rico.

Enslaved Indians search for gold in one of Puerto Rico's streams, as Spanish guards keep watch.

At first, the Taino welcomed the Spaniards. But the Spanish colonists forced the Taino—even children—to work long hours without pay. Taino dug for gold in Spanish mines on the island, planted and harvested the colonists' crops, and built roads and houses for them.

The Taino wanted to get rid of the Spaniards, but they had to be careful. They had never met people so different. And the colonists carried powerful weapons that were new to the Taino. Even so, the Indians began fighting back.

Taino men drown Salcedo in a river, proving that a Spaniard can be killed.

Sinking Salcedo

Most of what we know about the Taino in the 1500s was written by Spaniards hundreds of years ago. Experts believe that the stories may not be completely true.

Fact or fiction, this legend explains how Taino attacks on the Spanish soldiers began. According to several Spanish history books, the Taino believed that the Spanish people—with their unusual clothes and powerful weapons—could not be killed. Having never seen a Spaniard die, the Taino decided to test this belief and came up with a plan.

A group of them agreed to guide a Spaniard named Diego Salcedo across the island. When Salcedo and the Indians came to a river, the Taino offered to carry the Spaniard across the water. Midway, the Indians dropped Salcedo and held him under the water for several hours.

For the next few days, they watched the body to make sure he was dead. Once the news spread that a Spanish person could be killed, the Taino began attacking the Spaniards, hoping to drive away the unwelcome intruders.

Although the Taino outnumbered the Spanish settlers, the Indians carried only stone axes into battle. The axes were useless against the Spaniards' powerful swords and guns. Ponce de León and his men killed hundreds of Taino, including Gueybaná, one of the most powerful Taino caciques.

After the battle, few Taino remained on Puerto Rico. Many had already died from overwork or from diseases brought by the Spaniards. Others joined their old enemies, the Caribs, who were fighting the Spaniards on nearby islands. But a few Taino stayed and married Spanish settlers.

Between 1509 and 1512, Juan Ponce de León governed Puerto Rico.

Without the Taino to do their work, the Spaniards shipped people from Africa to Puerto Rico. The Spaniards forced the Africans to plant and harvest sugarcane, the colony's most important crop. Like the Taino before them, the African workers were slaves. By 1531 just over 400 Spanish settlers and more than 2,000 African slaves were living on Puerto Rico.

Slave traders traveled to Africa and kidnapped people to sell as slaves to Spanish landowners in Puerto Rico.

The British, led by Sir Francis Drake, attack a Spanish treasure ship. Great Britain wanted the riches the Spaniards gained from Puerto Rico and other American colonies. In 1595 Drake and his men unsuccessfully attacked El Morro.

The Spanish king allowed Puerto Rican settlers to trade only with Spain. This trade made the port city of San Juan an important stop for Spanish ships. But after Spain conquered other parts of America, Spanish ships did not stop very often on Puerto Rico. The traders could make more money from other colonies, which had more gold and silver.

But Puerto Rican colonists still needed food, clothes, tools, and other supplies to survive. So they illegally traded sugar, ginger, and other farm products in exchange for supplies from the French, British, and Dutch ships that anchored in Puerto Rico's ports.

The French, British, and Dutch wanted more from Puerto Rico than just sugar and ginger. They wanted some of the land that Columbus and other explorers had claimed for Spain. They also hoped to destroy Spain's power in the West Indies. In the 1500s and 1600s, France, Great Britain, and the Netherlands attacked Puerto Rico again and again.

To protect the port of San Juan, Spanish soldiers helped the colonists build a fortress overlooking San Juan Bay. Finished in 1540, the fortress was called La Fortaleza. Soon after, the Spaniards began building a second fort at San Juan named El Morro. Even with the new forts, Spain nearly lost Puerto Rico to the British and the Dutch. But the Spaniards proved stronger, and by 1625 they had driven away the attackers.

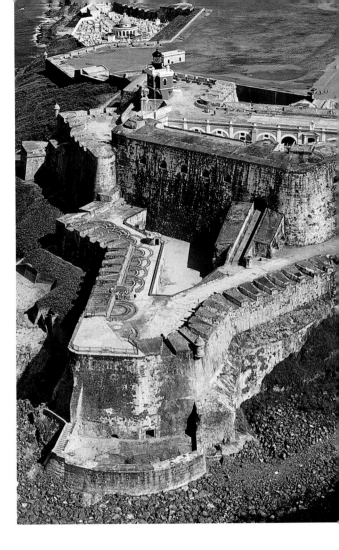

El Morro was the strongest fort in the West Indies for hundreds of years.

Spaniards used cannons to defend the forts of San Juan against enemy attacks.

Because Spain was a Catholic country, the Catholic Church played an important part in the lives of Puerto Rico's colonists. Monks and nuns ran the churches, cared for the sick, and taught reading, writing, and religion to some of the colonists' children.

During the mid-1700s, Spain's leaders encouraged settlers to move to Puerto Rico by giving away free land. Many Spaniards accepted this offer, and the colony's population began to grow rapidly. By 1765 nearly 45,000 people—including 5,037 slaves— lived in Puerto Rico's 24 towns. But the island still had only two schools. And because few roads led to outlying areas, only 5 percent of the land could be farmed. So the king of Spain ordered new schools and roads to be built. In addition, San Juan's forts were strengthened.

By the late 1700s, Puerto Rico's population had grown to more than 150,000 people. Some of the new residents had arrived with the Spanish navy and stayed to live on the island. Others came to find work. Some newcomers were former slaves who had run away from nearby Caribbean islands owned by other European countries.

With a mixture of Spanish, Taino, and African roots, Puerto Rican culture was changing. Taino words had crept into the Spanish language used by Puerto Ricans. African traditions and Caribbean music were also part of the Puerto Rican way of life. And Puerto Rico had become wealthier than it had ever been before.

Many Puerto Ricans were unhappy with Spanish rule. They wanted more control over their lives than the king of Spain permitted. Merchants sought freedom to trade legally with other nations. Many people wanted to lower the taxes they paid to Spain. Most Puerto Ricans wanted the freedom to elect their own government officials. And they wished for better schools and hospitals and for more roads and bridges.

In the late 1700s, coffee plantations flourished in Puerto Rico. Puerto Rico's mountains provided the perfect climate for this high-elevation crop.

Plantation owners who struck it rich built large, fancy homes surrounded by impressive gardens.

Around 1800 the countries of Spain, France, and Great Britain fought each other often. Because of these wars, the Spanish government did not have enough ships and soldiers to control its colonies. Spain began to allow Puerto Rico to trade with other nations, including the United States. The Spanish king also granted Puerto Ricans other freedoms.

In 1815 the king began to encourage people from outside Spain to settle in Puerto Rico. The new settlers, or **immigrants,** were given free land and did not have to pay taxes. This meant they could afford to plant vast fields of coffee beans, cotton, and cacao beans (for making chocolate) on **plantations,** or large farms.

Rafael Cordero ran a free school in his home from 1820 to 1868. Many of his students were the sons and daughters of poor plantation workers and slaves.

The new plantation owners needed more and more slaves to work in their fields. By 1850 the number of African slaves on the island had risen to 51,000. On neighboring islands, such as the British West Indies and the French Antilles, slavery had been outlawed. Puerto Ricans who opposed slavery tried to persuade the Spanish government to free Puerto Rico's slaves too. In 1868 Spain freed the children of Puerto Rican slaves. Spain ended slavery altogether in 1873, paying plantation owners for their loss of free laborers.

Luis Muñoz Rivera

In the late 1800s, Spain still did not allow Puerto Ricans to elect their own government officials. But in 1897, Puerto Ricans finally won the right to vote. The next year, they elected Luis Muñoz Rivera to lead the new government.

Just as the new government took office, Spain clashed with the United States and the Spanish-American War began. Within a few months, U.S. forces landed on the southern coast of Puerto Rico. On December 10, 1898, Spain surrendered Puerto Rico to the United States.

The United States government gave Puerto Ricans even less freedom than Spain had given them. At

first the U.S. military occupied the island and ran the Puerto Rican government. But by 1917, Puerto Ricans became U.S. citizens. That same year, the United States began allowing the people of Puerto Rico to elect some of their own government officials.

U.S. companies controlled much of the island's economy. For example, American businesses owned most of the island's sugarcane plantations and the mills that made the cane into sugar.

When the United States took over Puerto Rico, the U.S. military marched through San Juan.

35

Poorly paid Puerto Rican workers lived in dirty, crowded neighborhoods like this one in the early 1900s.

The companies paid very low wages to Puerto Rican workers. The sugar was sent to the U.S. mainland, where it was sold for huge profits—which benefited the companies but not the island's workers. Puerto Ricans earned so little money that by the 1920s, Puerto Rico was known as the Poorhouse of the Caribbean.

To improve the economy, the Puerto Rican government began a program in 1947 called Operation Bootstrap. Through this program, the government supplied more electricity so new factories could open.

Operation Bootstrap offered loans to businesses and encouraged foreign companies to move to Puerto Rico, creating more jobs for Puerto Ricans. Because of Operation Bootstrap, business grew and Puerto Ricans made more money.

At the same time, the U.S. government permitted Puerto Ricans to choose their own governor. In 1948 Luis Muñoz Marín, the son of Muñoz Rivera, was elected to the post. Muñoz Marín and several groups in Puerto Rico worked to reshape Puerto Rico's relationship with the United States. They also wrote a **constitution,** or set of basic laws, for Puerto Rico.

On July 1, 1952, the U.S. government approved the constitution for Puerto Rico. On July 25, Puerto Rico became the Commonwealth of Puerto Rico. But the new constitution and official name did not permanently settle questions about the future of the island.

Paper plants and other factories provided jobs to Puerto Rican workers in the late 1940s.

Puerto Rico's Choices

As a commonwealth:
Puerto Ricans . . .
* do not vote for U.S. president.
* do not pay U.S. federal taxes.
* study mainly in Spanish in school.

As a state:
Puerto Ricans . . .
* would vote for U.S. president.
* would pay U.S. federal taxes.
* would probably study in Spanish and English in school.

As an independent nation:
Puerto Ricans . . .
* would elect their own president.
* would pay their own federal taxes.
* would continue studying mainly in Spanish in school.

Above: The flags of Old San Juan, Puerto Rico, and the United States

Since the 1950s, Puerto Ricans have disagreed over what is best for the island. Some Puerto Ricans have wanted their island to become a nation independent of the United States. Others have argued that Puerto Rico should remain a commonwealth. Still others have favored making Puerto Rico a U.S. state.

In November 1993, Puerto Ricans voted on which of the three options they preferred. With most of its voters participating, Puerto Rico supported the commonwealth choice over the options of statehood or independence. In 1998 Puerto Ricans once again went to the polls to vote on the commonwealth's independence. Although about 46 percent voted in favor of statehood, 50 percent were undecided, so Puerto Rico remained a commonwealth.

As a commonwealth, Puerto Rico hopes to keep its ties to the United States, while preserving a strong sense of Puerto Rican culture. And Puerto Ricans will continue to discuss the best ways to improve life on their island.

The Rich Port

Murals add color to many Puerto Rican buildings.

or a long time, sugarcane, tobacco, coffee beans, and ginger were the mainstays of Puerto Rico's economy. But since Operation Bootstrap brought factories to Puerto Rico in the mid-1900s, manufacturing has become the island's most important industry.

Almost one out of every seven Puerto Rican workers is employed in the island's 1,800 factories. Some factory workers package medicines or assemble machinery or scientific instruments. Others sew clothes and leather goods, such as gloves and shoes. Still others make copper wire, television sets, rum, and cameras. At Puerto Rico's sugar mills, the island's sugarcane is processed into sugar.

A driver hauls harvested sugarcane to a mill for processing *(left)*. The island's most important fruit crop is bananas *(below)*.

Farms cover 60 percent of Puerto Rico's total land area. But only 3 percent of Puerto Ricans farm the land, and the value of the island's crops is small. Some farms produce milk, poultry, and eggs. Many farmers raise cattle for beef. In addition to sugar, coffee, and tobacco, fruits—such as bananas, pineapples, and coconuts—are grown on Puerto Rico.

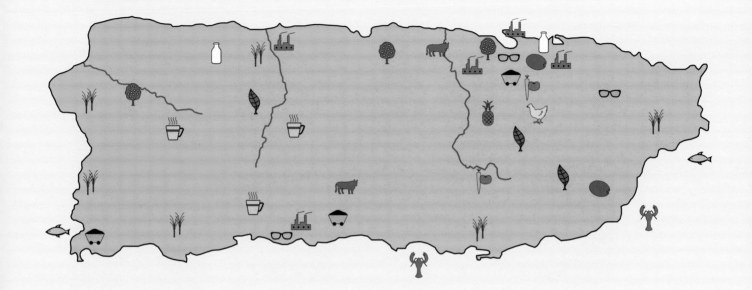

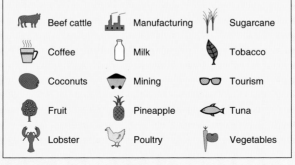

PUERTO RICO
Economic Map

The symbols on this map show where different economic activities take place in Puerto Rico. The legend below explains what each symbol stands for.

	Beef cattle		Manufacturing		Sugarcane
	Coffee		Milk		Tobacco
	Coconuts		Mining		Tourism
	Fruit		Pineapple		Tuna
	Lobster		Poultry		Vegetables

A San Juan fish vendor displays the catch of the day.

Some Puerto Ricans earn their living from the ocean waters. Fishers catch about 8 million pounds of fish and shellfish every year. Lobster and tuna are Puerto Rico's most valuable catches.

The government employs more than 20 percent of Puerto Rican workers. People working for the Puerto Rican government run government offices, teach in schools, and care for the sick in hospitals.

Teachers are important
service workers
in Puerto Rico.

U.S. government workers on Puerto Rico also serve in the military or protect wildlife in the Caribbean National Forest. Both the U.S. Navy and the U.S. Army have military bases on Puerto Rican land.

People who work in service industries make up more than half of Puerto Rico's workforce. Service workers sell goods or help people and businesses on the island. Clothing, medicines, and sugar are the most important goods that service workers buy and sell in Puerto Rico.

Many of Puerto Rico's service workers have jobs in tourism. Restaurant cooks, tour guides, hotel managers, and travel agents help the island's visitors enjoy their vacations. About 2.5 million tourists from the U.S. mainland and from around the world visit Puerto Rico every year.

Some of Puerto Rico's service workers have jobs in San Juan's Condado district. This area is popular for its beaches and hotels.

When tourists visit, they rub elbows with Puerto Rico's 3.8 million residents. Puerto Rico's large population squeezes into an area smaller than the state of Connecticut, making the island more crowded than any of the 50 states. Two out of every three Puerto Ricans live in the island's cities.

San Juan is Puerto Rico's capital and largest city. Long ago, the city spread beyond the walls the Spaniards had built to enclose it. The area surrounding San Juan includes the island's second largest city, Bayamón. Carolina, the third largest city, lies to the southeast of San Juan. Other large cities include Caguas and Ponce.

Puerto Rican Day parade in New York City

The ancestors of most Puerto Ricans were Spanish, African, and American Indian. But people from many other places have also settled on Puerto Rico. Some Puerto Ricans can trace their ancestry to Denmark, France, Great Britain, Germany, the United States, or Cuba. The island's ethnic mixture colors every part of Puerto Rican life, from music and art to religion and education.

Millions More on the Mainland

Puerto Rico has a large population, but in addition to the islanders, another 2 million Puerto Ricans live on the U.S. mainland. About half of these Puerto Ricans live in the New York City area. With such a large number of Puerto Ricans and other Latinos (people from Latin America), New York has several Spanish-language newspapers, radio programs, and television shows. The part of the city where many Puerto Ricans live—East Harlem—is known as *el barrío*, which means "the neighborhood" in Spanish.

Merrymakers in disguise celebrate the Fiesta de Santiago Apostol.

Fiestas, or festivals, are an important part of life on Puerto Rico. Every year each town on the island hosts its own religious fiesta, complete with parades, parties, and ceremonies. The Festival of San Juan, celebrated yearly on June 24, includes carnivals, dances, and music for several days before and after the holiday.

Musicians from around the world travel to Puerto Rico each year to play music at the Casals Festival. Held in San Juan, the festival is named in honor of Pablo Casals, a famous cellist who lived in Puerto Rico.

From this beach *(right)*, visitors can see San Juan's modern hotels built right next to a fort that's been there for centuries. Old San Juan *(below)* charms visitors with its narrow brick roads and brightly painted old buildings.

Visitors to San Juan can walk the narrow streets of Old San Juan, the section of the city that is still partially surrounded by walls. People can also visit the Church of San José, which was built in 1532. Or they can explore El Morro, the fort where Spaniards fought against enemy armies hundreds of years ago.

Art and music lovers will find many things to do in Puerto Rico. In the city of San Germán is a church called Porta Coeli (Gates of Heaven). Built in 1606, the church exhibits religious art. The Museo de Arte de Ponce (Ponce Museum of Art) displays the works of Puerto Rican and European artists. Plays, operas, and concerts are performed at the Centro de Bellas Artes in San Juan.

Divers love to explore
the reefs around
Puerto Rico.

Cockfighting is one of the most popular sports in Puerto Rico. In a cockfight, two cocks, or male chickens, attack each other. Many sports fans also enjoy the horse races at El Nuevo Comandante Racetrack.

Baseball, basketball, and boxing are also popular. Islanders enjoy baseball year-round, since their baseball season begins just as the U.S. mainland season ends. Some famous major-league players, such as Cleveland Indian Roberto Alomar and former Pittsburgh Pirate Roberto Clemente, began their careers in Puerto Rico.

Visitors examine the icicle-like rock formations that hang from the ceiling of a cave in Río Camuy Cave Park.

Many tourists visit Puerto Rico for the beaches and the warm, blue seawater surrounding the island. Deep-sea fishing, scuba diving, and swimming are popular activities throughout the year.

Off the island of Culebra, underwater snorklers discover colorful tropical fish darting through reefs of coral. Boaters and swimmers might spot a leatherback sea turtle, which can grow to almost seven feet long. Hikers can explore El Yunque in search of the rare Puerto Rican parrot.

Puerto Rico offers plenty of adventure underground, too. In Río Camuy Cave Park, located on northwestern Puerto Rico, tourists can hike along one of the largest underground rivers in the world. On Mona Island, visitors can explore caves that were once home to pirates. Perhaps a pirate even left a buried treasure behind!

THE ENVIRONMENT

Protecting the Parrots

uerto Rican parrots are hard to find. Their feathers are green, like the leaves of the trees in El Yunque—the rain forest where the birds live. The red spots on the birds' foreheads and the blue patches on their wings help a careful bird-watcher see the parrots. But the parrots are hard to find not only because they blend in so well with their surroundings but also because there are so few of them.

Christopher Columbus probably saw a lot of Puerto Rican parrots when he landed on Puerto Rico in 1493. Scientists think that as many as 1 million Puerto Rican parrots lived on the island at that time. Today only about 140 exist on the island.

Puerto Rican parrot

51

Puerto Rican parrots make their nests in the trees of El Yunque.

Though they are very rare, Puerto Rican parrots can still be spotted in the wild.

By learning how the parrots nest and raise their young, Puerto Ricans are trying to better understand what has happened to the birds since the Spaniards first settled on the island.

After a parrot chooses its mate, they both look for a big old tree in which to build their nest. They need a tree with a dry cavity, or hole, between 23 and 50 feet above the ground. In the nest, the female parrot lays two to four eggs. She then sits on her eggs for about one month. When the baby parrots peck their way out of the eggs, they are nearly featherless. But within nine weeks, the young birds have grown enough feathers to fly.

When Columbus landed on Puerto Rico, forests covered most of the island. Parrots could find plenty of large trees with cavities big enough for nests. But by 1912, as much as 80 percent of the forests on Puerto Rico had been cut down to make room for farms, towns, and cities.

The amount of forested land where parrots can nest is limited.

This **deforestation,** or clearing of forests, left the parrots with far fewer nesting trees. Parrots that could not find nesting places did not lay eggs. As a result, fewer baby parrots were born, and the parrot population dwindled. By 1940 Puerto Rican parrots could be found only in El Yunque.

Although the trees in El Yunque are big enough for parrot nests, the forest is much wetter than the forests in which the Puerto Rican parrots originally lived. Some of the tree cavities fill with water, making it impossible for the parrots to build nests in them.

Aerial views of Puerto Rico show land used for farming *(above)* and land devoted to development *(left).*

Artificial nesting cavities built by scientists provide safe places for parrots to make their homes.

Conditions can worsen in the summer and fall, when hurricanes threaten. These powerful storms rip through the forest, destroying nests and injuring or killing the birds.

Parrots also have had to compete with birds called thrashers and with bees from nearby farms. The thrashers and the bees also use tree cavities. By 1975 only 13 parrots were found living in El Yunque.

Since then scientists have been working to increase the number of parrots on Puerto Rico. Researchers have built artificial nesting cavities for the parrots to use. They have also built boxes for thrashers to nest in, leaving more natural cavities for parrot nests. Workers keep nesting places dry and clean and watch over the new parrot chicks to make sure they are safe and healthy.

Workers have also placed some parrot eggs in **incubators,** or heated containers that keep the eggs warm enough to hatch. Once the baby birds leave their shells and become strong, they live in protected **aviaries,** or large bird cages. Some of these parrots grow to adulthood and raise their young in the aviaries. Other birds are set free in El Yunque, where the parrot population has increased to more than 40.

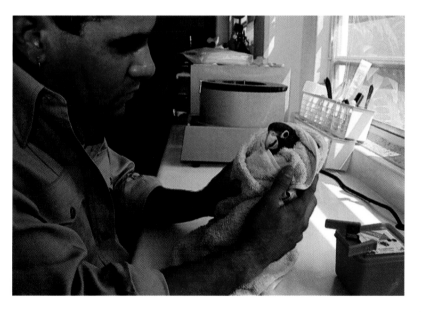

To help boost the population of Puerto Rican parrots, scientists raise baby parrots.

Wildlife experts take sick or injured parrots from the wild and put them in an aviary, where the birds are cared for until they heal.

When Hurricane Hugo struck the island in 1989, the wild population of birds was reduced to about 25 birds. Continued nurturing brought the parrot's population back up to 43 in the wild by 1998, when Hurricane Georges struck Puerto Rico. Fortunately, the area where most of the parrots nest suffered little damage. At least 36 of the 43 birds survived.

Efforts to increase the Puerto Rican parrot population continue. In 2000, 10 parrots were set free in El Yunque. And in 2001, 16 more parrots were released there. In the future, scientists plan to release some of the parrots in other forests on Puerto Rico.

This painting on the wall of a Puerto Rican school reminds students of the parrot's beauty and importance.

ALL ABOUT PUERTO RICO

Fun Facts

The world's largest telescope is at Arecibo Observatory in Puerto Rico. The telescope's reflector was built to cover a huge natural sinkhole.

The Milwaukee Deep, off Puerto Rico's northern coast, is one of the lowest places in the world. The underwater valley dips 28,000 feet below sea level.

Northeastern Puerto Rico is home to a part of the Caribbean National Forest that contains the mountain called El Yunque. The slopes of El Yunque have the only tropical rain forest in the United States outside of Hawaii.

El Yunque

At Mosquito Bay, off the island of Vieques, millions of tiny organisms in the water give off a strange glow. The bay becomes a dazzling light show at night. But this unique area is in danger of going dark. Pollution may kill off the glowing organisms. Environmentalists are trying to preserve the bay's glowing properties.

A kayaker explores Mosquito Bay.

Puerto Rico's capital city—San Juan—was originally named Puerto Rico, and the island itself was called San Juan. Historians believe that the names were switched by mistake on an early map.

Puerto Rico has two official languages, Spanish and English. Most Puerto Ricans speak Spanish at home and at work, but they begin learning English in kindergarten.

COMMONWEALTH SONG

LA BORINQUEÑA

Music by Felix Astol; lyrics by Manuel Fernandez Juncos

La tie-rra de Bo-rin quén don-de_he na-ci-do yo, es un jar-dín flo-

ri-do de má-gi-co pri-mor; mor; un cie-lo siem-pre ní-ti-do le sir-ve de do-

sel y dan a-rru-llos plá-ci-dos las o-las a sus pies. pies. Cuan-do_a sus pla-yas lle-gó Co-

lón ex-cla-mó lle-no de_ad-mi-ra-ción, ex-cla-mó lle-no de_ad-mi-ra-ción, Oh!

Es-ta_es la lin-da tie-rra que bus-co yo. Es Bo-rin-quén la

hi-ja, la hi-ja del mar y_el sol, del mar y_el sol. del mar y_el sol.

ENGLISH TRANSLATION

The land of Borinquén/Where I was born/Is a flowery garden/Of magical beauty;/
A sky that is always clear/Is like a canopy/And placid lullabies are sung/by the waves at her feet./
When Columbus arrived at her beaches/he exclaimed, full of admiration/Oh! Oh! Oh!/This is the
beautiful land/I'm looking for./It's Borinquén, the daughter,/the daughter of the sea and the sun,/
Of the sea and the sun,/Of the sea and the sun.

A PUERTO RICO RECIPE

Tostones are made from plantains, a banana-like fruit that is very common in Puerto Rico. Tostones can be served as an appetizer or as a side dish. They should be crispy on the outside and meaty on the inside.

TOSTONES

2 cups corn oil
3 green plantains

1. Have an adult help you peel and cut plantains into 1-inch diagonal slices.
2. In deep skillet, heat oil until very hot, but not smoking.
3. Have an adult help you carefully drop plantain slices into oil.
4. When plantains are brown on all sides, carefully remove with slotted spoon. Place between two pieces of waxed paper.
5. Flatten to ¼ inch thick.
6. Return plantain slices to hot oil. Refry until golden brown on all sides.
7. Remove with slotted spoon and drain on paper towels.

Serves 6 people.

HISTORICAL TIMELINE

A.D. 1000   Taino Indians build villages on the island that became known as Puerto Rico.

1493   Christopher Columbus claims Puerto Rico for Spain.

1511   Tainos Indians rebel against the Spaniards but are defeated.

1540   Workers finish La Fortaleza and begin building El Morro.

1818   The Spanish king awards free land to new settlers.

1873   Slavery is outlawed in Puerto Rico.

1895   The Puerto Rican flag is designed.

1897   Spain grants some self-governing powers to Puerto Rico.

1898   Spain surrenders Puerto Rico to the United States.

1917   Puerto Ricans become U.S. citizens.

1941   The U.S. Navy and Marines begin using part of the island of Vieques as a practice bombing range.

1946 Jesus T. Piñero becomes the first governor under United States rule.

1947 Operation Bootstrap, a plan to improve Puerto Rico's economy, begins.

1948 Luis Muñoz Marín becomes the first elected governor of Puerto Rico.

1952 Puerto Rico becomes a U.S. commonwealth.

1967 Puerto Ricans vote to remain a commonwealth.

1977 A major drought cripples the Puerto Rican economy.

1989 Hurricane Hugo hits Puerto Rico.

1993 Puerto Ricans vote again to remain a commonwealth.

1996 Hurricane Hortense hits Puerto Rico.

1998 Hurricane Georges sweeps across the island, causing $2 billion in damages. Puerto Ricans vote once again to remain a commonwealth.

2001 Hundreds of Puerto Ricans and Americans protest the U.S. Navy's bombing exercises on Vieques, fearing that the bombs put residents of the island in danger. President George W. Bush announces plans to end the bombing.

Roberto Alomar

Herman Badillo

Ramón Emeterio Betances

Roberto Clemente

OUTSTANDING PUERTO RICANS

Roberto Alomar (born 1968) is a baseball player from Ponce. Playing second base with the Toronto Blue Jays, he helped the team win the World Series in 1993. Winner of many Gold Glove Awards, Alomar began playing for the Cleveland Indians in 1999.

Herman Badillo (born 1929), from Caguas, Puerto Rico, is a politician who moved to New York City in 1941. He became the first Puerto Rican to be elected to the U.S. Congress. He served in the House of Representatives from 1971 to 1977. Badillo has headed the Governor's Advisory Committee on Hispanic Affairs in New York since 1983.

Ramón Emeterio Betances (1827–1898) was a doctor and social reformer. He worked to rid Puerto Rico of diseases such as cholera and led the fight to outlaw slavery. Betances was from Cabo Rojo, Puerto Rico.

Pablo Casals (1876–1973) was a world-famous cellist, composer, and conductor who moved from Spain to Puerto Rico in 1956. Casals founded the Puerto Rico Symphony Orchestra and began the Casals Festival—a yearly musical event in San Juan that attracts musicians and music lovers from around the world.

Roberto Walker Clemente (1934–1972), of Carolina, Puerto Rico, was one of baseball's greatest players. As an outfielder for the Pittsburgh Pirates, he earned the Gold Glove Award 12 times. Clemente died in a plane crash. Soon after, he was elected to the National Baseball Hall of Fame.

José Feliciano (born 1945) moved from Lares, Puerto Rico, to New York City, where he began his musical career in the early 1960s. Born blind, he taught himself to sing and to play many musical instruments. In 1968 Feliciano won Grammy Awards for best male pop singer and for best new artist. Many people know his popular Christmas song, "Feliz Navidad."

José Feliciano

Gigi Fernández (born 1964), a world-class tennis player from San Juan, was named the Puerto Rican Female Athlete of the Year in 1988. She won the U.S. Open doubles championship in 1988, 1990, and 1992. In 1992 Fernández and her partner won Olympic gold medals in doubles tennis. In 1997 Fernández retired from tennis after losing the U.S. Open doubles championship.

Gigi Fernández

José Ferrer (1912–1992), the star of many films and stage productions, was born in Santurce, Puerto Rico. In 1950 he won an Academy Award for his role in *Cyrano de Bergerac*. Ferrer became a member of the Theater Hall of Fame in 1981.

Eugenio María de Hostos (1839–1903), born in Río Cañas, Puerto Rico, wrote a variety of books including children's stories and the novel *La Peregrinación de Bayoán*. Hostos also fought to provide a free education for all Puerto Rican children.

José Ferrer

Raúl Juliá (1940–1994) was an actor from San Juan. His many roles included Count Dracula in a Broadway production and Rafael the Fixit Man on television's *Sesame Street*. Julia also starred in the films *Presumed Innocent* and *The Addams Family*.

Raúl Juliá

René Marqués

Ricky Martin

Concha Meléndez

Rita Moreno

René Marqués (1919–1979) was a playwright and short-story author from Arecibo, Puerto Rico. His most famous play—*La Carreta*—was first performed in 1953 and was published in 1961. The play came out in English as *The Oxcart* in 1969.

Ricky Martin (born 1971) first gained fame in the Latin pop group Menudo. He dabbled in acting before becoming an international singing sensation. He is well known in the United States for his hit song "Livin' La Vida Loca." Martin was born in San Juan.

Concha Meléndez (1892–1990) was a well-known poet. She also wrote many books and essays about the works of famous writers from different Latin American countries. Meléndez was born in Caguas, Puerto Rico.

Rita Moreno (born 1931) is an actress, dancer, and singer from Humacao, Puerto Rico. She is probably best known for her role as Anita in *West Side Story*. Moreno is the only woman ever to win all four of the entertainment world's highest awards—she has an Oscar, a Grammy, a Tony, and two Emmys.

Luis Muñoz Marín (1898–1980), born in San Juan, was the first elected governor of Puerto Rico, serving from 1948 to 1964. Muñoz Marín helped develop Operation Bootstrap, a plan to spur Puerto Rico's economy. He also set up Puerto Rico's commonwealth relationship with the United States.

Luis Muñoz Rivera (1859–1916), the father of Muñoz Marín, was a newspaper editor and politician from Barranquitas, Puerto Rico. He worked with Spanish officials and later with the U.S. government to gain more rights for Puerto Ricans.

Antonia Coello Novello (born 1944) from Fajardo, Puerto Rico, is a well-known leader and researcher in the field of children's health. In 1989 she became the first person of Latino roots and the first woman to be named U.S. surgeon general.

Antonia Coello Novello

Francisco Oller y Cestero (1833–1917), one of Puerto Rico's most famous artists, completed more than 800 paintings during his long life. Many of Oller's works portray his antislavery views. The artist from Bayamón also painted Puerto Rican landscapes.

Felisa Rincón de Gautier (1897–1994) was born in San Juan, where she served as mayor from 1946 to 1968. Named Woman of the Year in the Americas in 1954, she presided over the Inter-American Organization of Municipalities the same year.

Francisco Oller y Cestero

Juan ("Chi Chi") Rodríguez (born 1935), from Río Piedras, Puerto Rico, became a professional golfer in 1960. Since then, Rodríguez has been one of the most popular and talented golfers in the United States.

Lola Rodriguez de Tío (1854–1924), from San Germán, wrote poetry and songs, including a version of the Puerto Rican anthem, "La Borinqueña." Her longest work, *Mis Cantares*, is a collection of 2,500 poems.

Felisa Rincón de Gautier

Arthur Schomburg (1874–1938), from San Juan, moved in 1891 to New York, where he led black cultural groups and began a collection of documents from African American history. The collection, which Schomburg later oversaw at the New York Public Library, was named after him upon his death.

FACTS-AT-A-GLANCE

Nickname: *Isla del Encanto* (Island of Enchantment)

Song: "La Borinqueña"

Motto: *Joannes est nomen ejus* (John Is His Name)

Flower: *maga*

Tree: ceiba (kapok)

Bird: *reinita*

Became a commonwealth: July 25, 1952

Capital: San Juan

Area: 3,435 square miles

Average January temperature: 73° F

Average July temperature: 80° F

Puerto Rico's flag, designed in 1895, was officially adopted in 1952. It is very similar to Cuba's flag.

POPULATION GROWTH

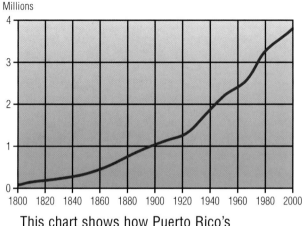

Millions

This chart shows how Puerto Rico's population has grown from 1800 to 2000.

The lamb that appears on Puerto Rico's seal symbolizes peace and brotherhood. Other symbols on the seal refer to Puerto Rico's history as a Spanish territory.

Population: 3,808,610 (2000 census)

Major cities and populations: (2000 census) San Juan (421,958), Bayamón (203,499), Carolina (168,164), Ponce (155,038), Caguas (88,680)

U.S. senators: 0

U.S. representatives: 1, nonvoting

Natural resources: clay, gravel, rivers, salt, sand, soil, stone, warm and moist climate

Agricultural products: avocados, bananas, cattle, citrus fruits, coconuts, coffee, eggs, honey, pineapples, plantains, poultry, sugarcane

Fishing industry: oysters, lobsters, tuna

Manufactured goods: clay, clothing, electronics equipment, food products, glass products, leather products, machinery, medicines, stone

WHERE PUERTO RICANS WORK

Services—54 percent (services includes jobs in trade; community, social, and personal services; finance, insurance, and real estate; transportation, communication, and utilities)

Government—23 percent

Manufacturing—14 percent

Construction and mining—6 percent

Agriculture—3 percent

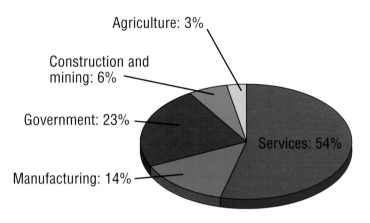

GROSS STATE PRODUCT

Services—45 percent

Manufacturing—41 percent

Government—11 percent

Construction and mining—2 percent

Agriculture—1 percent

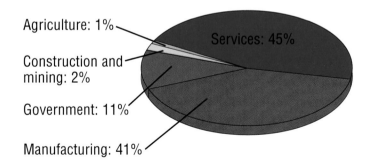

PUERTO RICO WILDLIFE

Mammals: bat, guinea pig, mongoose, Puerto Rico Paso Fino horse

Birds: booby, bullfinch, nightingale, flycatcher, *gorrion*, grosbeak, parrot, *pitarre*, plover, Puerto Rican pigeon, Puerto Rican whippoorwill, reinita, sandpiper, tanager, tern, thrush, warbler

Reptiles and amphibians: coquí, gecko, iguana, lizards, snakes

Plants: African tulip, barrel cactus, breadfruit, ceiba (kapok), coconut palm, ebony, *flamboyan*, *guanabana*, laurel, mahogany, orchid, organ pipe cactus, papaya, poinsettia, star apple, sea grape

Fish: barracuda, butterfly fish, herring, lobster, marlin, mullet, oyster, parrot fish, pompano, puffer fish, red striped grouper, shark, snapper, Spanish mackerel, tuna

Iguana

PLACES TO VISIT

Caguana Indian Ceremonial Park, near Utuado
Visitors can learn about the life of the Taino at this important Taino ceremonial center. The ruins date from A.D. 1200.

El Morro Fortress, San Juan
Explore the tunnels and dungeons of this old fort. The Spanish built El Morro in stages between 1539 and 1787 to guard the bay of San Juan.

El Yunque rain forest, in the Caribbean National Forest
Take a hike through this 28,000-acre rain forest and listen for the song of the coquí frog.

Hacienda Buena Vista, near Ponce
This restored coffee plantation and grain mill dates from the 1800s. The mill and the plantation's main building are open for tours.

Las Cabezas de San Juan Nature Reserve, near Fajardo
Sandy beaches, rock cliffs, coral reefs, islands, dry forests, mangrove trees, and lagoons can all be found here. Laguna Grande is one of the three glowing lagoons in Puerto Rico.

Mosquito Bay, near Esperanza
At this bay along the coast of Vieques, microorganisms in the water absorb sunlight during the day and then glow after dark. Unfortunately, the bay is threatened by pollution.

Museo de Arte de Ponce

This is where you'll find the Caribbean's most extensive art collection. Exhibits feature art from Puerto Rico and from European countries.

Museo de las Americas, San Juan

Find out more about life in North, Central, and South America through the centuries. Look for the colorful collection of carnival costumes.

Río Camuy Cave Park, near Arecibo

Take a trolley-tram ride into one of the more than 200 caves in this northeastern Puerto Rico park. The largest underground river in the world, the Camuy River, carved the caves.

San Juan Museum of Arts and History, Old San Juan

This museum, once a marketplace, houses a collection of Puerto Rican art. To learn more about San Juan, watch the video about the city's history.

Sun Bay, on Vieques Island

Swim and sun here. It's one of the island's most popular beaches and picnic areas.

A beach near Sun Bay

ANNUAL EVENTS

Three Kings' Day, San Juan—*January*

Carnaval, Ponce—*February*

Dulce Sueño Paso Fino Horse Show, Guayama—*February–March*

Bomba y Plena Festival, Ponce—*June*

Casals Festival, San Juan—*June*

San Juan Bautista Day, San Juan—*June*

Fiesta de Santiago Apostol, Loíza—*July*

Indian Festival, Jayuya—*November*

Puerto Rican Music Festival, San Juan—*November–December*

Patron Saint Festival, Las Marías—*November–December*

LEARN MORE ABOUT PUERTO RICO

BOOKS

General

Davis, Lucile. *Puerto Rico.* New York: Children's Press, 2000.

Levy, Patricia. *Puerto Rico.* New York: Marshall Cavendish, 1995.

Special Interest

Aliotta, Jerome J. *The Puerto Rican Americans (Immigrant Experience).* New York: Chelsea House Publishing, 1995. This book tells the story of Puerto Ricans in the United States. It examines their history and their struggle to be accepted, yet maintain a separate cultural identity.

Kaufman, Cheryl Davidson. *Cooking the Caribbean Way.* Minneapolis: Lerner Publications Company, 2002. Provides recipes from all of the islands in the Caribbean, including one for a Puerto Rican stew called *asopao*.

Perez, Frank and Anne Weil. *Raúl Juliá.* Austin, TX: Raintree Steck-Vaughn, 1996. This biography traces the 30-year career of the well-known Puerto Rican actor.

Sauvain, Philip. *Rain Forests.* Minneapolis: Carolrhoda Books, Inc., 1996. Explores the rain forest environment, including the diverse range of plants and animals that thrive there. The text also delves into threats to rain forests.

Souza, D. M. *Hurricanes.* Minneapolis: Carolrhoda Books, Inc., 1996. Souza explains how these fierce wind and rain storms form. Color photographs illustrate the damage they have caused in Puerto Rico and in other coastal areas.

Walker, Paul Robert. *Pride of Puerto Rico: The Life of Roberto Clemente.* San Diego: Harcourt Brace & Company, 1988. In this biography of Roberto Clemente, readers learn more about the Puerto Rican hall-of-famer who played right field for the Pittsburgh Pirates.

Fiction

Jaffe, Nina. *The Golden Flower: A Taino Myth from Puerto Rico.* New York: Simon & Schuster, 1996. This Taino folktale explains through words and color illustrations how water came to be on Earth.

Mohr, Nicholasa. *Going Home.* New York: Puffin Books, 1999. Mohr tells the story of an 11-year-old Puerto Rican American girl who returns to the island to visit relatives.

Mohr, Nicholasa. *The Song of El Coquí and Other Tales of Puerto Rico.* New York: Viking, 1995. These three illustrated folktales high-light the storytelling traditions of Puerto Rico.

WEBSITES

El Boricua
<http://www.elboricua.com/>
The website of El Boricua is an online monthly bilingual publication for Puerto Ricans. It features news articles, information about upcoming events, Puerto Rican recipes, and a page for kids.

Welcome to Puerto Rico
<http://welcome.topuertorico.org/>
This website is a great source for general information about the commonwealth, including island geography, wildlife, and culture.

The Caribbean National Forest
<http://www.r8web.com/caribbean/>
Provides information about the plants and animals found in El Yunque and posts a calendar of special events in the park.

PRONUNCIATION GUIDE

Arecibo (ah-ray-SEE-boh)

Bayamón (bah-yah-MOHN)

Caguas (KAH-gwahs)

Cordillera Central (kor-dee-YEH-rah
 sen-TRAHL)

Culebra (koo-LAY-brah)

El Yunque (el YOON-kay)

Muñoz Marín, Luis (MOON-yohs mah-
 REEN, loo-EES)

Ponce de León, Juan (POHN-say day
 lay-OHN, HWAHN)

San Juan (SAHN HWAHN)

Sierra de Luquillo (see-EHR-rah day
 loo-KEE-yoh)

Taino (TAY-noh)

Vieques (vee-AY-kehs)

GLOSSARY

aviary: a large cage or building for keeping wild birds in captivity

colony: a territory ruled by a country some distance away

commonwealth: a territory (or other political unit) that has power over its own local affairs but that is voluntarily tied to a larger nation through shared laws and rights. The Puerto Rican term for commonwealth, *estado libre asociado,* means associated free state.

constitution: the system of basic laws or rules of a government, society, or organization, and the document in which these laws or rules are written

deforestation: the large-scale cutting or burning of trees and other plants in a forest

immigrant: a person who moves into a foreign land and settles there

incubator: a container equipped with heat and lights to keep bird eggs warm enough to hatch

plantation: a large estate, usually in a warm climate, on which crops are grown by workers who live on the estate. In the past, plantation owners usually used slave labor.

tropical rain forest: a thick, wet, evergreen forest with annual rainfall of more than 100 inches. Tropical rain forests are located in hot, wet climates near the equator.

INDEX

PHOTO ACKNOWLEDGMENTS

Cover photographs by Wolfgang Kaehler/CORBIS (left), Bob Krist/CORBIS (right). Digital Cartographics, pp. 1, 8, 9, 42; Suzanne Murphy-Larronde, pp. 2-3, 75; Doug Perrine/Innerspace Visions, p. 3; Tony Arruza, pp. 4 (detail), 7 (detail), 17 (detail), 40 (detail, right), 45, 51 (detail, left), 52; Marvin W. Schwartz, p. 6; NE Stock Photos: © Margo Taussig Pinkerton, p. 10, © Jim Schwabel, p. 55 (right); © Thomas R. Fletcher, pp. 11, 12, 13, 14, 15, 16 (right), 30, 41 (right), 48 (left), 54, 80; JAIME LAURENO/AQUA GRAPHICS/CHICAGO, pp. 16 (left), 49, 50; Vanni Archive/CORBIS, p. 18; Puerto Rico General Archives, pp. 19, 24, 25, 27, 32, 34, 36, 37, 66 (second from bottom), 68 (top, second from bottom), 69 (middle, bottom); Puerto Rico Federal Affairs Administration, p. 20 (left); Leslie Fagre, p. 20 (right); Independent Picture Service, p. 21; Bodleian Library, University of Oxford, p. 22; Knights of Columbus Headquarters Museum, p. 23; *Dictionary of American Portraits*, p. 26; Bettmann/CORBIS, p. 28; Mark Bacon, p. 29; James L. Amos/CORBIS, p. 31; Archives of the Audio-Visual Unit/Art Museum of the Americas/OAS, p. 33; National Archives, Neg. no. 126-PG-5G-9, p. 35; Wolfgang Kaehler, pp. 38, 60, 73; © W. Lynn Seldon, Jr., p. 40; Eugene G. Schulz, pp. 41 (left), 43, 44, 48 (right), 55 (left); Owen Franken/CORBIS, p. 46; Tony Arruza/CORBIS, p. 47; U.S. Fish and Wildlife Service: Tomas Carlo, p. 51, Jose Colon, p. 53, Jafet Velez, pp. 56, 57, 59, Luther C. Goldman, p. 58; Frank Borges Llosa, p. 61; Tim Seeley, pp. 63, 71 (top), 72; Toronto Blue Jays Baseball Club, p. 66 (top); Herman Badillo, p. 66 (second from top); Pittsburgh Pirates, p. 66 (bottom); RCA Records, p. 67 (top); Carol Newsom, p. 67 (second from top); Hollywood Book & Poster, p. 67 (second from bottom, bottom); Mitchell Gerber/CORBIS, p. 68 (second from top); Kenneth G. Lawrence's Movie Memorabilia Shop of Hollywood, p. 68 (bottom); Office of the U.S. Surgeon General, p. 69 (top); Jean Matheny, p. 70.